THE RISK OF BREXIT

ABOUT POLICY NETWORK

Policy Network is an international thinktank and research institute. Its network spans national borders across Europe and the wider world with the aim of promoting the best progressive thinking on the major social and economic challenges of the 21st century.

Our work is driven by a network of politicians, policymakers, business leaders, public service professionals, and academic researchers who work on long-term issues relating to public policy, political economy, social attitudes, governance and international affairs. This is complemented by the expertise and research excellence of Policy Network's international team.

A platform for research and ideas

- Promoting expert ideas and political analysis on the key economic, social and political challenges of our age.
- Disseminating research excellence and relevant knowledge to a wider public audience through interactive policy networks, including interdisciplinary and scholarly collaboration.
- Engaging and informing the public debate about the future of European and global progressive politics.

A network of leaders, policymakers and thinkers

- Building international policy communities comprising individuals and affiliate institutions.
- Providing meeting platforms where the politically active, and potential leaders of the future, can engage with each other across national borders and with the best thinkers who are sympathetic to their broad aims.
- Engaging in external collaboration with partners including higher education institutions, the private sector, thinktanks, charities, community organisations, and trade unions.
- Delivering an innovative events programme combining in-house seminars with large-scale public conferences designed to influence and contribute to key public debates.

www.policy-network.net

THE RISK OF BREXIT

Britain and Europe in 2015

Roger Liddle

ROWMAN & LITTLEFIELD
INTERNATIONAL
London • New York

Published by Rowman & Littlefield International, Ltd.
Unit A, Whitacre Mews, 26-34 Stannary Street, London SE11 4AB
www.rowmaninternational.com

Rowman & Littlefield International, Ltd. is an affiliate of Rowman &
Littlefield
4501 Forbes Boulevard, Suite 200, Lanham, Maryland 20706, USA
With additional offices in Boulder, New York, Toronto (Canada), and
London (UK)
www.rowman.com

British Library Cataloguing in Publication Information Available
A catalogue record for this book is available from the British Library

ISBN: PB 978-0-9928705-5-3
ISBN: electronic 978-0-9928705-6-0

Library of Congress Cataloging-in-Publication Data

Liddle, Roger.
The risk of BREXIT : Britain and Europe in 2015 / by Roger Liddle.
pages cm.
ISBN 978-0-9928705-5-3 (pbk. : alk. paper) — ISBN 978-0-9928705-6-0 (electronic) 1.
Great Britain—Politics and government—2007- 2. European Union—Great Britain. 3. Great
Britain—Foreign relations—European Union countries. 4. European Union countries—
Foreign relations—Great Britain. I. Title.
JN238.L53 2015
341.242'20941—dc23
2014048869

Printed in the United States of America

CONTENTS

v

ABOUT THE AUTHOR

Roger Liddle is chair of Policy Network and became a life peer in 2010. He was formerly Tony Blair's special adviser on European policy and subsequently worked for three years in the European commission, first in the trade commissioner's cabinet and then advising the president of the commission. He has been at the heart of the Europe debate for two decades, with detailed knowledge of both the politics and public policy.

Roger has written extensively on European and British affairs, including *The Blair Revolution* (with Peter Mandelson, 1996), *Global Europe, Social Europe* (with Anthony Giddens and Patrick Diamond, 2006) and *Beyond New Labour* (with Patrick Diamond, 2009), and most recently *The Europe Dilemma: the Drama of EU Integration* (IB Tauris, 2014), as well as several other Fabian Society and Policy Network pamphlets.

He also co-authored two papers for the president of the European commission's thinktank, the Bureau of European Policy Advisers, on Europe's Social Reality (February 2007) and the Single Market: Yesterday and Tomorrow (July 2006), and since then has contributed to various edited collections on the single market, the social challenges facing Europe, the case for a social investment strategy and Britain's European policy.

INTRODUCTION

2015 will be a critical year for Britain and Europe.

One known certainty is that there will be a British general election in May. On its highly unpredictable outcome, given massive public disillusion with a fragmenting two-party system, much will hang for Britain's future relationship with the European Union.

One near certainty is that David Cameron will only remain prime minister if he can deliver a parliamentary majority for his stated European policy: a fundamental renegotiation of Britain's relationship with Europe and an in/out referendum by the end of 2017. The paradox here is that Britain's EU membership is not an issue that, according to opinion polls, the British public would put anywhere near top of the list of their priorities. It is the internal politics of the Conservative party, against the background of the rise of the UK Independence party, that has forced Cameron into this corner over Europe. Yet, how he manages to deliver this unbreakable pledge to his own side will have an important bearing on the eventual European outcome. A Cameron premiership with a confident overall majority will be different to a Cameron premiership constrained by a continuing coalition with Nick Clegg's pro-European Liberal Democrats. A Conservative minority government would be torn in different directions if it depends for votes of confidence on special deals with handfuls of populists (Northern Ireland's Democratic

Unionists and Ukip members of parliament) or successfully cuts a constitutional deal for radical home rule with the Scottish nationalists.

Another near certainty is that if Ed Miliband ends up as prime minister, despite Labour's weakening lead in the polls and negative ratings, an in/out referendum will not feature in Labour's first Queen's speech. Miliband has been resolute that on grounds of principle as well as political priorities for Britain, he will oppose such a course. However, if Labour is in government, its position in both parliament and the country is likely to be weak: a second general election in short order may be on the horizon. A defeated Conservative party, in all likelihood under a new leader, would shift further in an anti-European direction. Also, Ukip may have emerged in the 2015 general election as the main alternative to Labour in many of the party's traditional heartlands. Instead of a Europe referendum in 2017 under the Conservatives, the election of a Labour minority government could lead to a further UK general election in 2016 or 2017, in which Europe and immigration would remain opposition obsessions and might be the trigger for a major political realignment. One way or another, the election of a Labour government will not bury the European question for the foreseeable future.

2015 will also be a critical year for the European Union, in which decisions central to Europe's future will be taken. It will be a critical year for European recovery and the future of the euro: can Europe's policymakers establish a new consensus on economic policy to revive growth? It will be the first full year of Jean-Claude Juncker's European commission. The European institutions committed themselves in the summer of 2014 to an ambitious reform agenda: in 2015, we will get an impression of whether they are serious. Can old deadlocks be broken and new grand bargains made to give new impetus to the single market? This will be critical to the credibility of the 'reform' agenda that commands all party consensus in the UK. Finally, the security threats around the EU's borders – nationalism in Russia, fanaticism in the Middle East, chaos in North Africa – will test Europe's unity of purpose and relevance. All of these developments will have an important bearing on how the EU is perceived in Britain and how the case for and against our EU membership is made. In the memorable title of Anthony Nutting's 1960 pro-European tract, 'Europe will not wait' while the British political class duck and weave over our membership.

In my own recent book, *The Europe Dilemma*, I described the story of Britain's relationship with the Europe as a drama in three acts. The first act is a half century of 'Missed Opportunity', from Britain's failure to participate in the Schuman plan in 1950, to the paralysing indecisiveness on European questions of the closing years of the Major government. The second act is 'Blair's Failure': the story of how Tony Blair and Gordon Brown initially both wanted to resolve the semi-detachedness and half-commitment in Britain's relationship with Europe, but for a variety of reasons, many their own fault, they fell out and failed. The third unfinished act I titled 'Cameron's Gamble'. The book analyses the evolution of Conservative policy towards Europe, up to and including the in/out referendum pledge that Cameron made in his January 2013 Bloomberg speech. That pledge, which the prime minister made in an otherwise well-argued speech on the future of the European Union, was a double defeat for Cameron. First, it was a pledge he had never wanted to make. Second, he only made it in the deluded belief that the pledge of an in/out referendum in 2017 would kill the European question as a divisive issue inside the Conservative party for the remainder of the 2010-15 parliament. That has proved a major miscalculation.

This extended essay fills out the continuing drama of 'Cameron's Gamble'. The first chapter serves as a reminder of the political background to the emergence of Cameron's renegotiation/referendum policy and explains why he felt he had no alternative but to make this pledge. The second analyses the imprecise and moving target of what the detailed agenda of a Conservative renegotiation might eventually be. The third chapter reflects on the likely acceptability of this agenda to our EU partners, how much importance they attach to continuing British membership and how much political capital in the rest of the EU David Cameron can call upon to achieve his objectives. Chapter four discusses the politics of a referendum and what conditions would be necessary for the public to endorse a positive outcome of a Conservative renegotiation. The fifth chapter considers prospects for the May 2015 general election. The sixth asks what would and should be different if a Labour-led government is formed. The final chapter concludes.

HOW WE GOT HERE

The Remorseless Logic of Conservative Division on the European Question

The promise of an in/out referendum on Britain's EU membership was something that David Cameron never wanted to make. When he ran for the Conservative leadership in 2005 a central part of his analysis of why the Conservatives had lost three successive general elections was their perceived obsession with Europe. In his first speech as leader to a Conservative conference in October 2006, he could not have been more emphatic:

'Instead of talking about the things most people care about, we talked about what we cared about most. While parents worried about childcare, getting the kids to school, balancing work and family life – we were banging on about Europe.'

Since going into opposition in 1997, the Conservatives had struck highly Eurosceptic positions, opposing the ratification of every single one of the four European treaties that the Labour government signed and making the commitment that under the Conservatives, Britain would 'never' join the euro. Cameron's objection was not apparently to the substance of these positions, but to the priority the Conservatives had given them in their campaigning and public image. On the issue of substance, no one quite knew where he stood. No one imagined he was a pro-European enthusiast. As a young man, he had joined Conservative central office in the late 1980s at a point when Margaret Thatcher's Bruges speech had set a new, more sceptical tone. He then worked as a special adviser for leading Eurosceptics Norman Lamont and Michael Howard. Yet for all that, it is difficult to believe that someone of his naturally conservative disposition, rooted in his comfortable stockbroker background in the Berkshire countryside, would see his place in history as defying the view of the British national interest taken by every single British prime minister since Harold Macmillan, and leading Britain out of the European Union.

The Conservatives still stood on the ground defined by both parts of the slogan that William Hague had coined in 1999, 'in Europe, not run by Europe'. No one disputed that there existed within their ranks what was often dismissed as a strong anti-European 'fringe'. However, the 'fringe' now penetrated to the 'core' with the cabinet itself containing a significant number of hardcore sceptics. At the height of the eurocrisis, James Forsyth, the respected Spectator columnist, estimated that nine Conservative cabinet members were perfectly relaxed about the possibility of UK withdrawal.

Cameron himself presented an ambiguous stance. As prime minister, Cameron refused to reverse his decision to withdraw Conservative MEPs from the European People's party group in the European parliament. Instead they formed the European Democrat grouping of anti-integrationist MEPs, along with the Polish Law and Justice party and others from mainly small eastern European parties, among whose number were members with an unsavoury antisemitic and homophobic past. Cameron had made the pledge to pull the British Conservatives out of the EPP under duress in the early stages of the Conservative leadership election of 2005. He did it in order to win over a crucial handful of Eurosceptic MPs who had been supporters of Liam Fox (who was to become Cameron's short-lived first defence secretary). Yet it was telling that Cameron proved unwilling to reverse this commitment, despite the very real loss of credibility and influence in Europe that his decision caused. Not only did Cameron preclude his party from major roles in the European parliament, he equally excluded himself from the influential, regular leaders' meetings that always precede European councils.

His decision greatly upset the German Christian Democrats, including Angela Merkel personally, who set great store by the development of pan-European political links between 'respectable' centre-right parties with a pro-EU, pro-social market orientation. In response Cameron launched a charm offensive with the German chancellor, which initially seemed to have convinced her that he genuinely wanted to keep Britain in the EU. This relationship is fundamental to any prospect of keeping Britain within the EU, but UK internal politics continue to subject it to a bumpy ride.

The reason is simple. With his activists Cameron has chosen to avoid a direct challenge to their prejudices and assumptions: on Europe there was nothing to compare, for instance, with how he had chosen to handle matters of lesbian and gay equality. Cameron must always have been aware of the risk he was running inside the Conservative party on the European question: that at some point, an EU development of some kind would cause Europe to come back as an issue to haunt the Conservatives. But his short-termist mindset led him to take the risk of assuming nothing dramatic was in prospect that would threaten the weak consensus in support of British membership that had been established in the UK after Blair's failure to take Britain into the euro. Despite his evident admiration for Blair, he did not follow Blair's example over clause IV, in deliberately engineering a battle within his party to rid it of one of the most damaging shibboleths that weakened both its public credibility and its capacity to govern.

Cameron entered office with little political capital in the bank. For all his strength of personality, his natural presence and command, and Gordon Brown's weakness as his opponent in the 2010 election, the Conservatives failed to win an overall majority. His leadership failed the ultimate test of politics. In 2010, the Conservative share of the vote on 36 per cent was some 6-8 per cent lower than the 42-44 per cent share the Conservatives consistently won from when Margaret Thatcher last ejected Labour from office in 1979 to when the Conservatives had last won a general election under John Major in 1992. In the aftermath of the inconclusive election result, Cameron moved swiftly to enter into a five-year coalition agreement with the Liberal Democrats – without the wider party consultation that his coalition partners undertook. Arguably the fragile state of the economy required a strong and stable government, which to a remarkable degree the coalition has managed to provide. However, this was not Cameron's only option: an alternative would have been to form a minority government as the largest party and hold another general election within a year or so. This would have followed the precedent of Harold Wilson who had formed a minority government in similarly grave economic circumstances in February 1974 and went on to win a small overall majority in a second general election that October. Many Conservatives would have preferred Cameron to have taken that risk. Few accepted the leadership's argument that the government of the country was strengthened by the very act of forming the coalition. Dislike of the coalition was commonplace at the party grassroots and among MPs outside the Cameron/Osborne 'magic circle', particularly those disappointed by their failure to secure office. Dislike of the constraints that their Liberal Democrat coalition partners were assumed to impose on the government's European policy was part of the reason.

Before 2010, Cameron's desire to 'stop banging on about Europe' had been helped by events. By the late 2000s, Europe had faded as a political concern. The Conservative attempt to demand a referendum on the Lisbon treaty between 2007 and 2009 never really took off. Europe barely featured as an issue in the 2010 general election. Cameron was sensitive, however, to how far the creation of the coalition disappointed Conservative Eurosceptics. The Lisbon treaty's final ratification by all 27 member states came six months before the British general election, scuppering his own firm pledge to hold a referendum on it. President Václav Klaus of the Czech Republic ignored the pleas of British Eurosceptics to delay his signature on the treaty until after the UK election. While David Cameron had made a well-publicised personal appeal to Klaus, the Czech president's firm rejection of his entreaties must have been a genuine relief. Conservatives rested on William Hague's enigmatic promise that if Lisbon was ratified before the Conservatives came to office, the new government 'would not let matters rest there'. To this end, the Conservative manifesto had pledged to 'repatriate' limited powers from Brussels, but this was abandoned in the coalition agreement. Instead the coalition merely committed to examine the 'balance of competences' between Britain and the EU. Yet Eurosceptics must have known that, even before the election, allies of David Cameron and William Hague had been briefing that the commitment to repatriation of powers would not be an 'early priority' for them for fear of setting off an immediate confrontation with EU partners. For the Conservative leadership, the coalition with the Liberal Democrats was a convenient excuse for inaction.

The coalition's major concession to Eurosceptic opinion was the European Union Act 2011, introducing a so-called 'referendum lock' on any future transfers of power to Brussels. This measure passed through parliament with little resistance, except from pro-Europeans in the House of Lords. The Act reflected the prevailing received wisdom, shared by the leadership of all three main parties, that the Lisbon ratification should draw a firm line under any further EU treaty change. Such institutional navel gazing, it was confidently asserted, would be unnecessary for a generation: Brussels already had more than enough powers and certainly did not need more.

The explosion of the eurozone crisis overturned these complacent assumptions. It faced the Conservative leadership with a tough choice. Many Conservatives welcomed the prospect of a breakup of the hated euro: there arose a united chorus of voices gleeful with *schadenfreude*, insisting that their principled objections to the euro had been proved right. Former Conservative chancellors Nigel Lawson and Norman Lamont powerfully reinforced these arguments. However to his credit, George Osborne, the current chancellor, mounted a brave response that it was in the interests of the British economy and banking system for eurozone cataclysm to be avoided.

Osborne sought to sugar this pill for his Eurosceptic party with a clever argument that became the driving idea behind Cameron's original concept of renegotiation. In the chancellor's view, the 'remorseless logic' of the further eurozone integration necessary to make the single currency viable for the long term, would require the negotiation of a major new European treaty. This would establish a more fiscally federal and democratically accountable eurozone. Britain would never be part of this more integrated currency area. However, as part of this process of inevitable treaty revision, Britain as a euro-outsider would then be able to negotiate a 'looser relationship' within the EU. At the same time, Britain would insist on robust protections against unfair discrimination by the 'euro-ins' to the disadvantage of the 'euro-outs'.

The chancellor's decision to put so much stress on the 'remorseless logic' of eurozone integration also served a wider political purpose. He was setting up a binary choice about the future of the euro: on the one hand, the high degree of economic and political integration within the eurozone that was an assumed inevitability made membership impossible for any British government; on the other, it was perfectly possible for the UK to remain in a looser EU outside a federalised inner core. A two-tier Europe was unavoidably emerging that would require a thorough institutional rethink for all EU members. Through this inevitable evolution, Britain could negotiate a new relationship and a 'new settlement'.

Osborne's logic was, however, a revolutionary proposition in terms of 40 years of British European policy: for the first time, the UK was arguing for the establishment of a two-tier Europe in which Britain would exclude itself voluntarily from the inner core and be content to be consigned to a looser outer ring, simply sharing the single market with eurozone partners. Among Eurosceptic Conservative MPs, the prospect on offer was of freedom from being locked into a remorseless escalator to a super state: yet outside Conservative ranks, it felt more like relegation to Europe's second division.

Of course, the eurozone crisis had some short term political upsides. It offered the government convenient cover for Britain's continuing economic difficulties and an explanation for their failure to meet their ambitious fiscal targets. It also enabled the coalition to support from the sidelines the ongoing rescue of the euro, though this was done in a way calculated to exasperate EU partners. Fierce public criticism of the eurozone's slowness in taking decisive action was combined with point blank private refusal to offer or underwrite a cent of financial support for the various rescue packages (except for a bilateral loan to Ireland). The UK gave its approval to the small treaty change necessary to set up the European stability mechanism. Yet Conservative backbenchers criticised the government's failure to use the leverage offered in order to secure progress on the repatriation of powers. The increasingly heated politics of the Conservative party culminated in a near-farcical UK 'veto' of the fiscal treaty in December 2011, seen as essential by Merkel to secure German public support for the euro rescue: the farce was that the treaty went ahead as an intergovernmental treaty outside the formal EU structure with only the UK and Hungary refusing to sign up. Use of the 'veto' was seen to have practical limits.

As the eurozone crisis dragged on, it added to the government's medium-term political problems on Europe. First, it brought back the European question with its full divisive force. In part this was because the eurozone's handling of the crisis undoubtedly undermined public support for EU membership. Earlier generations had in part been persuaded that Britain had no alternative but to 'join Europe' because on economic growth, the continental record had, until the 1990s, far outshone its own. Now the public saw on their television screens constant witness to a failing and divided Europe. The never-ending drama played out in the media of the euro crisis in 2011 and 2012 – the absence of any single clear step towards its resolution, the endless succession of summits in Brussels which never appeared to do enough, banking collapse in Ireland, the political crisis in Italy, civil disturbance in Greece and Spain – conveyed an image of chaos, confusion and deep woe. The whole European project seemed on the point of collapse. Understandably, the British public were horrified and it was no surprise that support for EU withdrawal rose in opinion polls. (The significance though of this shift should not be exaggerated: there was a similar period during the 'Eurosclerosis' of the early 1980s when a clear UK majority in the opinion polls favoured withdrawal.)

Second, the salience of Europe as a political issue offered the oxygen of publicity to the UK Independence party, which took full advantage of the opportunity. Paradoxically, the Ukip surge was a different side of the same coin as the Liberal Democrats becoming a party of government for the first time in generations. As the Liberal Democrats surrendered their position as the third-party receptacle for midterm protest votes, Ukip gained a considerable midterm boost in the 2010 parliament, culminating in their emergence as the largest party in the May 2014 European parliamentary elections, their first parliamentary byelection victory in Clacton, Essex in October 2014 and the possibility of further byelection triumphs and near-misses.

The rise of Ukip has had a profoundly disturbing effect on the Conservative party base. Conservative party membership has collapsed from 2.5 million of the 1950s to not much more than a 100,000 today. As a result, Conservative MPs owe their position in parliament to a 'selectorate' of Conservative activists which is much less representative of 'middle Britain' than in earlier decades. The remaining activists are, in the main, middle class, elderly, non-cosmopolitan in outlook and out of touch with the social currents of modern Britain. This was vividly illustrated on the issue of same-sex marriage in the early months of 2013: an issue which aroused seething discontents among Conservatives, but on which public opinion was much more relaxed. That is why since the early 1990s, it has become virtually impossible to win a Conservative constituency selection without striking a Eurosceptic posture.

Several reasons explain this strong hostility to the EU among Conservative activists. A minority opposed Britain's European Economic Community membership from the very start and many sympathised with the positions taken by Enoch Powell in the late 1960s and early 1970s. However, the major shift to Euroscepticism took place in the early 1990s. The severity of the early 1990s recession was blamed on British membership of the Exchange Rate Mechanism. The lasting aftershocks of Thatcher's deposition reinforced the view that she 'had been right all along' about Europe. This message was constantly reiterated by what the political scientist

Tim Bale describes as the 'party in the media' preaching an ideological Thatcherism in which the myth of her consistent hostility to Europe played a crucial part. Since Thatcher, the party's leaders have commanded less loyalty and respect because they have been less electorally successful, in part because that very same 'party in the media' severely constrained their freedom of manoeuvre to modernise the party.

The gut instinct of the depleted Tory base is that Ukip is made up of natural allies and friends who should return to their true home. With the rise of Ukip (under its charismatic leader, Nigel Farage) these instincts have grown stronger, as Ukip has branched out from its anti-European core to campaign on issues like immigration, welfare and gay marriage. The Conservative party 'base' blamed the absence of 'sufficiently strong' Conservative policies, particularly on Europe and immigration, for the success of the Ukip insurgency: the promise of an in/out referendum seemed the obvious panacea. Not only would it help the Conservatives ward off the undoubted Ukip threat in European elections, but the more considerable risk of vital votes in Conservative marginal seats draining away in a general election.

The explosion in Conservative Euroscepticism came in many shapes and sizes, both in motive and aim. The Conservative parliamentary party had always contained a group of anti-European 'last ditchers' who objected to our EU membership on grounds of sovereignty. Yet hostility to Europe brings together a number of different and broader ideological currents – from old fashioned xenophobes, anti-immigration populists and 'little Englanders' to more sophisticated critiques from neocons, libertarians, and 'hyperglobalisers' who see the EU as holding Britain back. These were joined by sceptics of many stripes and hues who wanted to see a fundamental change in the nature of the relationship between Britain and the EU: many professed a desire to remain members of the EU, but there was a huge question mark over the realism of the conditions on which they imagined this to be possible. Their only point of unity was an increasing vocal chorus in favour of an in/out referendum.

This rumbling volcano in an unmodernised Conservative party first erupted into public view in a Commons vote on a backbench motion calling for a referendum on Britain's continued EU membership on 25 October 2011. No fewer than 81 Conservative backbenchers defied a (clumsily imposed) three-line whip to vote against a referendum, a far larger rebellion than any there had been on Maastricht ratification in the early 1990s. And the ranks of the rebels extended well beyond what one might describe as the anti-European 'last ditchers'. They included able young backbenchers from the 2010 intake, whom one would normally expect to be loyal to the whip in the hope of future office. They may have acted from high motives of conviction or the low calculation of pleasing constituency activists in reselections to come. However, it also showed that many backbench Conservatives believed the momentum behind a referendum was unstoppable and that the leadership would eventually be forced to bend to this demand, or, if it did not, the party leadership itself would not survive.

The October 2011 vote gave the call for an in/out referendum irreversible momentum inside the Conservative party. David Cameron's 'veto' of the fiscal treaty at the December European council in the same year reflected in part a political calculation that he could not carry a ratification bill through the Commons without huge pressure to amend it to include an in/out referendum. As the eurozone began to debate the necessary measures to ensure full completion of economic and monetary union in the first half of 2012, the supporters of a referendum assumed their moment had finally arrived. When, at the June council later that year, David Cameron appeared to dismiss a referendum at his press conference the storm of protest on the backbenches became such that he was forced to concede in a newspaper article the following day that in his mind the words 'Europe' and 'referendum' went together. From then on, all that had to be written was the language and argument of his Bloomberg speech.

THE SHIFTING RENEGOTIATION AGENDA

For Eurosceptics and anti-Europeans, what really mattered about Cameron's Bloomberg speech was his unconditional commitment to an in/out referendum by the end of 2017. Cameron's primary concern appeared quite different: to sketch out an agenda for his proposed renegotiation that had a plausible chance of success and enable him to argue that his intention was for Britain to remain in a 'reformed' EU.

However, by the time he came to formalise his referendum pledge in January 2013, the 'remorseless logic' of comprehensive treaty change that George Osborne had taken as a given when the eurozone crisis exploded in 2010 no longer had the same air of inevitability about it – or at least it was no longer on Cameron's 2017 timetable. Since autumn 2012, the eurozone crisis calmed. No one would claim it had been 'solved', but temporarily at least the eurozone had stabilised. The problems of the eurozone moved from being systemic to chronic. The European Central Bank has interpreted its mandate, under Mario Draghi's leadership, with boldness not foreseen when the institution was first established in 1999, remarkably in spite of the resignations of the two most senior German members of its executive board. In addition, major integrative steps have been taken to tighten fiscal discipline, to establish the European stability mechanism and to build a banking union, all by stretching the existing treaty framework or, in the case of the fiscal treaty, agreeing a new intergovernmental treaty outside it.

So far, the need for comprehensive change in the existing EU treaties has been avoided. Few of our eurozone partners are keen to address the evident democratic deficit in the new governance arrangements they have agreed. For one thing, there is no consensus over what further eurozone integration means; for another, there is a desperation to avoid the political problem of new treaty ratification that could well require national referendums on an unpopular EU in some member states. This is a particularly unappealing prospect for François Hollande in the present political conjuncture in France. Ironically, the only member states that agree with the British preference for comprehensive treaty change are at present Belgium and Italy from their traditionally federalist perspectives. But unless the eurozone suddenly appears once again on the point of collapse, no dramatic move for a major new treaty looks likely before 2017.

Stymied by the lack of EU enthusiasm for comprehensive treaty change, Cameron and Osborne changed tack and argued that their top priority was a reform agenda for the whole EU. In the Bloomberg speech, Cameron set out a wide-ranging reform agenda, pitched to appeal to continental as well as British opinion. His speech called for a more flexible, adaptable and democratically accountable EU, focused on competitiveness, with power flowing back and forth between the member states and Brussels and with a greater role for national parliaments in its governance. Its thrust struck a real chord in many member states.

In truth, the Bloomberg speech was couched in more positive terms about Britain's membership of the EU than any speech made by a Conservative leader since John Major's 'heart of Europe' speech in Bonn in 1990. The peroration hit emotional highs worthy of one of Tony Blair's better European speeches:

> When the referendum comes, let me say now that if we can negotiate such an arrangement I will campaign for it with all my heart and soul.

> I believe something very deeply. That Britain's national interest is best served in a flexible, adaptable and open European Union and that such a European Union is best with Britain in it.
> Over the coming weeks, months and years, I will not rest until this debate is won.

The bulk of the speech, however, was a characteristically British argument that, while the EU had massive historical achievements to its credit, it now needed to change and reform. Cameron's 'vision for a new European Union, fit for the 21st century' was built on 'five principles' well-honed to appeal to business opinion, much of the continental centre-right, and 'northern liberals' of all mainstream political persuasions:

Competitiveness

Completing the single market should be 'our driving mission'. The EU should urgently address 'the sclerotoic, ineffective decision making that is holding us back'.

Flexibility

'We must not be weighed down by a one-size-fits-all approach that implies all countries want the same level of integration'. The 'essential foundation' of the EU is the 'single market rather than the single currency'. In place of ever-closer union, the British had a vision for the EU's future based on 'flexibility and cooperation – [that] is just as valid'.

Power must be able to flow back to member states

'Let us not be misled by the fallacy that a deep and workable single market requires everything to be harmonised ... Countries are different. They make different choices ... We need to examine whether the balance is right in so many areas where the European Union has legislated including on the environment, social affairs and crime.'

Democratic accountability

'We need to have a bigger and more significant role for national parliaments ... in the way the EU does business.'

Fairness

'Whatever new arrangements are enacted for the eurozone they must work fairly for those inside it and out.' That is why 'Britain has been so concerned to promote and defend the single market as the eurozone crisis rewrites the rules on fiscal coordination and banking union.'

Cameron justified his decision to back an in/out referendum on the basis that it was now inevitable:

> Public disillusionment [in Britain] with the EU is at an all-time high ... People feel the EU is heading in a direction they never signed up for ... They resent interference ... by what they see as unnecessary rules and regulations ... They feel the EU is heading for a level of political integration that is far outside Britain's comfort zone.
> I believe in confronting this issue – shaping it, leading the debate . . . not simply hoping a difficult situation will go away.

Despite the referendum pledge, such was the positive tone of Cameron's speech that it led to a rise in public support for Britain's EU membership, a movement of opinion that also coincided with the easing of the eurozone crisis. Among the governing and opinion-forming classes and within the business community, his speech induced a spirit of complacency about the risks of Brexit. Despite Cameron's concession of a referendum, most imagined that from a pro-European point of view it would somehow 'work out alright on the night': Cameron would be able to cobble together with our EU partners some superficially attractive renegotiation deal and the public would follow an all-party and business lead advocating a vote to stay in.

Eurosceptics inside the Conservative party reacted quite differently. The absence of a convincing prospect of major treaty change undermined the credibility of Cameron's concept of a 'fundamental renegotiation of Britain's EU relationship' with the traditional Eurosceptics in his party. Their preferred model for future British membership is limited to a polity that (at least as far as the UK is concerned) is based on no more than free trade and intergovernmental cooperation. They see the European question in terms of a stark choice between membership of a body that is evolving inexorably in the direction of a federal superstate and a free trade area of friendly nations which is much looser than at present. No other member state shares this aspiration for the EU, nor do any of our partners accept the reality of the stark choice that invigorates the British Eurosceptic imagination. In the eyes of our partners, to pose this stark choice betrays a poor understanding of the complex polity of multi-level governance that the EU has become, which operates as a hybrid of intergovernmentalism and supranationalism over specific policy domains where member states have decided that the benefits of pooled sovereignty outweigh its national loss.

Also, the Eurosceptic view that the EU should fundamentally be about 'free trade' dismisses the essentially political foundations of the European project. It also fundamentally misunderstands the nature of the 'single market', which represents a far higher degree of economic integration 'behind the border' than can simply be achieved through free trade.

For these reasons, David Cameron may be quite relieved that comprehensive treaty change is not in prospect. British Eurosceptics would have little chance of achieving what they claim to want. His political problem remains, however. Eurosceptics tend to assume that Britain can renegotiate anything it wants, as long as the government shows sufficient toughness. They exaggerate Britain's bargaining power inside today's EU. By convincing themselves that threats to leave will be sufficient to obtain their unrealistic demands, they are complacent about the risks of ending up outside, shut out from the 'free trade' benefits to which they attach such priority. Cameron's problem is that many of his sceptics, who may currently imagine themselves as voting in a referendum to stay in, are a long way from understanding these realities.

Yet from their perspective, with the very promise of a renegotiation, Eurosceptics have already won an important victory. David Cameron is the first British prime minister since Harold Wilson to have argued that the existing basis for our membership is unsustainable (though in the 'I want my money back' budget clashes of the early 1980s, Margaret Thatcher may have come pretty near). It is one thing to call for 'reform' of the EU: quite another to imply that without 'reform', Britain might be better off outside. Cameron has been extremely opaque on this point (one might say shifty, if this was not unkind): he insists his demands for EU reforms will be met and has so far used refused to say what course he would recommend if his renegotiation fails. This political line will prove difficult for him to sustain in the coming months: in his immigration speech on 28 November 2014, Cameron headed off the pressures to say that in some circumstances he could recommend a no vote with the elliptical phrase 'if our concerns fall on deaf ears, I rule nothing out.' In this May's election campaign he will be pressed hard to spell out in more detail what this might mean.

The inherent difficulties Cameron faces became fully apparent in the summer of 2014. Ukip emerged top of the poll in the European parliamentary elections on 22 May. The unanimous view of political analysts is that the explanation for Ukip's remarkable success was far more complex than anything simply to do with Europe. In polling, concerns about immigration featured far more. Ukip constantly played on the link between public concerns about immigration and our EU membership, because of the EU treaty commitment to 'free movement'. These concerns became more salient with the flood of publicity about the consequences of the end of transitional controls on free movement from Bulgaria and Romania in January 2014. For Conservative Eurosceptics (for whom Ukip is seen either as an existential threat or a potential ally because it is campaigning on what should be 'their' territory) the issue of curbing 'free movement' soared to the top of their agenda for Cameron's EU renegotiation. The rest became a side issue.

The Conservatives were able to stall the Ukip bandwagon with a convincing win in a byelection in Newark on 5 June 2014. However, Ukip gained unexpected new momentum with the defection of the Conservative backbencher Douglas Carswell to their ranks and his overwhelming victory as the Ukip candidate in a byelection in his seaside constituency of Clacton, Essex on 9 October. The shock of Carswell's defection transmuted into fear of a Conservative pre-election meltdown when, on the eve of their 2014 annual conference, Carswell was joined by Mark Reckless, MP for Rochester and Strood on the north Kent coast, who went on to capture the seat for Ukip in November.

At that moment, Britain stepped much nearer the fatal edge in its dangerous 'sleepwalk to exit' from membership of the European Union. Under electoral pressure from Ukip, the defection of two Conservative MPs to Nigel Farage's populists, and the rumoured threat of even more to come, the Conservative party leadership hardened its rhetoric and announced a major change in the government's EU negotiating strategy.

Political rhetoric is a currency of little solid worth. But an interview between the prime minister and the Today programme's Jim Naughtie on 30 September marked a significant change of tone from the Bloomberg speech. Naughtie began by recollecting that Cameron had said he would be 'heartbroken' by the breakup of the United Kingdom if the Scots had voted yes to independence in the September 2014 referendum. He then asked how Cameron would feel if Britain voted to leave the EU. Cameron, in a show of mock surprise at the question, replied that he cared 'a thousand times more strongly' about the campaign to keep Scotland in the UK. 'The United Kingdom was an issue of heartbreak. This is a position of pragmatism: how do we get the best deal for Britain. That's what I feel strongly about.' Something fundamental had happened to his Bloomberg statement about Europe that he would campaign for Britain's EU membership 'with all [his] heart and soul'.

In his conference speech the same week, Cameron emphasised a single new focus for his renegotiation: 'the biggest issue today is migration from within the EU'. He declared that the issue of migration would be 'at the very heart of my renegotiation strategy'. Looking straight into the TV cameras, he solemnly pledged: 'Britain, I know you want this sorted. I will go to Brussels, I will not take no for an answer. When it comes to free movement, I will get what Britain needs.'

Cameron's Conservative conference speech marked a crucial change. A mere 21 months earlier at Bloomberg, Cameron had set out a plan for renegotiation that involved a series of reforms that were in the interests of the whole EU. Now, the question of migration and free movement, which had not even been mentioned in the Bloomberg speech, (except to warn Britons that the rights that hundreds of thousands took for granted to live, work and retire on the continent could no longer be guaranteed if we left) took centre stage. This was the culmination of a gradual hardening of Cameron's statements on free movement in response to Ukip's success and the growing salience of immigration. Initially the prime minister had talked about tighter numerical controls on, and longer transition periods for, migration from newly acceding member states with much lower income capita than western countries. Next, in advance of the European elections, the Conservatives had pledged to crack down on 'benefit tourism' and refuse permission to settle in Britain to EU migrants who failed to find jobs. But in his conference speech Cameron went much further. According to Cameron, 'the biggest issue today' is not just abuses of welfare but 'numbers that have increased faster than we in this country wanted [. . .] at a level that was too much for our communities [and] for our labour markets'. The only common sense interpretation of his language is that he was pledging to curb the numbers of EU migrants coming to the UK, whether they were able to find jobs or not. Admittedly in his November 2014 immigration speech, Cameron stepped away, in the face of pressures from Brussels and the German chancellor Angela Merkel, from his 'red line' of imposing quotas on EU migrants coming to Britain, in favour of restricting the ability of migrants to stay here without a job and reducing the incentives for lower-paid, lower-skilled workers to come here in the first place by imposing new requirements that those who want to claim tax credits and child benefit must live here and contribute to our country for a minimum of four years.

Less than a month after his conference speech, Cameron found himself forced into another destructive row over British contributions to the EU budget. Cameron claimed that only two days before the October meeting of the European council he had discovered that Britain was being required by the European commission to make a back payment of £1.7bn to the EU budget as a result of a statistical adjustment to the calculation of Britain's annual national income stretching back a decade or more. He insisted that Britain would not pay the bill by the time demanded and that a special meeting of finance ministers be called to discuss its justification. He won some support for this from other member states, particularly the Netherlands and Italy, who were also hit by the adjusted back charge.

This was a classic EU row. The commission saw itself as implementing a set of rules on annual budgetary adjustments that member states had unanimously agreed, based on estimates of national income provided by independent national statistical offices under definitional guidance given by Eurostat: no British official had apparently flagged up a problem in advance, despite the fact that the UK Office for National Statistics had warned back in the spring that the revised gross national income estimates submitted to Eurostat would have implications for Britain's payments to the EU budget. The British, on the other hand, saw themselves as victims of a continental conspiracy: an unaccountable European commission and an unfair penalty on Britain's economic success. Cameron first said he would refuse to pay and then said only that he would not pay by 1 December 2014. At a meeting of finance ministers on 7 November, Osborne secured a delay in the payment until July 2015 and claimed that he had halved what was due, owing to the face that the British rebate would apply to the additional contribution. A climbdown had taken place but only at the larger cost of a further souring of our EU relations.

Of course, a political case can be mounted in Cameron's defence. He had little alternative to be tough on immigration and the budget if the two high-profile Tory defections to Ukip were not to be followed by a steady stream of others, fatally undermining Conservative chances in the general election. Yet, while David Cameron and George Osborne clearly want Britain to stay in Europe, the question is whether – assuming they remain in government after the general election in May 2015 – they have the political strength, or more accurately the political courage, to make good on their clear preference. Cameron has moved a long way from his 2006 statement that, if the Conservatives were to modernise their appeal, they had to stop 'banging on about Europe'. Even when forced into making his referendum pledge, he claimed it would enable the government to get on the front foot on Europe, as he put it at Bloomberg: 'confronting this issue – shaping it, leading the debate'. But it is clearly evident that in the last two years it is Ukip and his anti-European backbenchers who have been leading and shaping Britain's European debate. And he has been forced into a complete about turn on his renegotiation strategy in a desperate attempt to head off Ukip. These pressures are not going to go away; the tragedy for Cameron is that his offer of an in/out referendum appears only to have strengthened them.

WILL OUR EU PARTNERS DELIVER WHAT CAMERON NEEDS?

How will our EU partners respond to Cameron's demands for 're-negotiation'? How much do they care about British membership? The dominant mood in Brussels and among our partners is one of extreme irritation with Cameron, almost bordering on contempt, for what they see as a cavalier stance on Europe, driven purely by domestic politics. Yet for all that, underneath this *froideur*, a rational analysis suggests that it remains strongly in the interests of our partners to try hard to keep Britain as members. In a speech in London in October 2014, the outgoing president of the commission, José Manuel Barroso, argued that Britain would count for little in the world if it left the EU. He may well be right. But at the same time, the EU itself would be diminished – seriously, but not fatally – without the UK's economic weight, global reach and vision, transatlantic affinity and military capability.

Even in France, where the positive history of the *entente cordiale* has often been marred by Gaullist truculence, Anglo-Saxon rivalry and genuine differences in attitude towards the US, there is increasing recognition on both sides of the channel that the global interests of the two nations are now historically aligned. There may be some Parisian resentment about the success of the City of London and a broader sense of French upset about the number of their citizens migrating to work in the UK. However, it is far-fetched to think that France would happily see the back of Britain with its departure from the EU in the hope that some internationally mobile banks and finance houses might shift their location across the Channel. French hopes of making Europe a powerful force for good in the world, which they can they help lead, depend for their realisation on active partnership with the British. Germany lacks the same post-imperial global outlook.

Of course, there are strong integrationists (and not just in France) like Michel Rocard, the socialist intellectual and former prime minister of France, who believe Britain has for most of its 40 years of membership proved a 'ball and chain' around the neck of closer union. Federalists complained bitterly that the constitutional treaty (torpedoed by the French and Dutch referendums in 2005) was a 'British text' and the complaint was made even more loudly about its Lisbon treaty substitute that was eventually ratified in 2009. But to paint the British as the main political obstacle to the advance of EU integration has been discredited by the recent eurozone experience. As a non-euro member, the UK is in a weak position to block integrationist progress. Yet the failure of the eurozone crisis to result, so far at least, in a new radical institutional settlement, suggests that the UK is far from being the only member state standing in the way of closer union. Rather it suggests that in the past the UK has acted as an instinctive sceptic of grand schemes and 'Europe for Europe's sake' proposals, behind whom other equally reluctant member states have been only too glad to hide.

British influence has contributed at times to some of the costly mistakes the EU has made. For example, as a result of the UK's success prior to 2008 in pressing for liberalisation of wholesale financial markets (though this was the mood of the age) at the same time as resisting the development of adequate EU-wide regulation. But the same could be said of France's reluctance to contemplate radical reform of the common agricultural policy or Germany's stubborn refusal to take advantage of its economic freedom of manoeuvre to expand domestic demand. For the most part, the British have brought pragmatic common sense to the EU's counsels. When the UK commits to action at EU level, it tends to deliver, for example in implementing the '1992 programme' for the internal market.

Yet obviously, continuing British membership, for all that it brings to the EU, cannot be secured 'at any price' in terms of the EU's long-term policy goals and institutional integrity. The frustration with Cameron in Brussels and national capitals is not because of a point blank refusal to contemplate the idea of renegotiation, rather it has been the British government's opaqueness in spelling out what its precise renegotiation objectives are, combined with an increasingly populist bluster of 'noises off' from London. Our partners' frustration is that the 'reform' agenda that Cameron advocated in his Bloomberg speech is actually making progress. Cameron could argue, if he chose, that most of his reform objectives are contained within the five-year plan agreed between the European council and the incoming commission president, and endorsed in principle by the European parliament. Indeed, the opportunity of a new commission appointed at the start of a new European parliament's five-year term should have been celebrated as the golden opportunity to set Europe on a new course.

The British government wasted this opportunity to proclaim a fresh start by a mishandled row over the appointment of Jean-Claude Juncker as the new commission president. It may have been legitimate for the British to object strongly to the *Spitzenkandidaten* (lead candidate) process for choosing the next president. It may also be understandable to argue that Jean-Claude Juncker is not a convincing symbol of the EU seizing the mantle of reform: as prime minister of Luxembourg, he has been around for far longer than any other current European leader and is a classic creature of Benelux coalition building and compromise. However, the publicity given to Cameron's opposition to Juncker's appointment, while helpful to him in the short term with Conservative MPs, has been counterproductive in terms of highlighting the opportunity that now exists to achieve real reform under the new commission. The evidence for this sense of opportunity lies in the individual quality of the commissioners, Juncker's internal reorganisation of the commission to streamline its focus on key objectives, and clear policy commitments in areas such as the digital single market and the single market in services. In addition, Juncker set aside any sense of personal affront to give Cameron's nominee as British commissioner, Jonathan Hill, responsibility for financial services, which remains a key UK national interest. Indeed, it may not be such a bad thing from a UK point of view to have a Benelux fixer in charge of the European commission: after all, it is the only EU institution that commands the right of legislative initiative over any policy item in Cameron's renegotiation agenda, which might require new EU directives or an amendment to existing directives. It is possible that just as Hermann Van Rompuy, a former Belgian prime minister, gained enormously in stature in his term of office as president of the European council from 2010–2015, Juncker may do the same.

Nor is some treaty change a totally lost cause for Cameron. Any changes agreed would have to be limited (probably under what in the Lisbon treaty is described as the 'simplified revision procedure', which avoids the need for a full-blown process of treaty revision and the calling of a convention). They could not be of a nature that would require a referendum in other member states. Yet there could be some significant changes. For example, the Germans have hinted at one such possible concession to British sensibilities: stronger legal guarantees of protection against discrimination by 'euro-ins' against 'euro-outs'.

Cameron may also succeed in securing one or two symbolic treaty opt-outs for the UK. Winning one or two opt-outs could be regarded as today's equivalent of the additional quotas for cheap New Zealand lamb and butter that Harold Wilson skilfully trumpeted in the 1975 referendum. But negotiability will all depend on the nature of the opt-outs he chooses to press for. Some years ago, the preferred Conservative choice would have been to reinstate, in some new form, the opt-out from the social chapter that John Major negotiated at Maastricht in 1991. But British business today seems less exercised than it once was on this point. One possibility might be to seek an opt-out from the working time directive to the UK, which was never covered by the original opt-out, but again the practical impact and value of such a change is uncertain. Also, for symbolic reasons, it might be a difficult concession to win. The French – and perhaps others – would argue that such an opt-out could give the UK an unfair competitive advantage in European markets. Also opt-out concessions for the UK could put some continental leaders under pressure from their own Eurosceptics: right-wing populists would doubtless argue that if the UK can get out of its EU obligations, the same should be possible for them. The strength of the populist showing in the European elections can only have reinforced this political problem.

In the first 18 months following his Bloomberg speech, Cameron played his renegotiation cards close to his chest. In an article for the Telegraph in March 2014, he offered some 'detail of the specific changes' he would seek in Britain's relationship with the EU, which the newspaper summarised as seven targets for change. At the party conference in October 2014, the Conservatives significantly toughened the rhetoric and substance of their positions on free movement of labour and the European convention on human rights.

In ascending order of negotiating difficulty, Cameron listed his renegotiation demands as follows:

New powers for national parliaments

Powers for national parliaments to issue 'yellow card' warnings about proposed EU legislation already exists in the Lisbon treaty. These could be beefed up without treaty change. One possibility is that the role of Cosac, the body that represents the EU committees of national parliaments, could be boosted so that it can give earlier warning of impending new legislation to national parliaments and their committees and better coordinate the 'yellow card' responses to new proposals provided for in the Lisbon treaty. Cameron has so far been clear that it is collective action by a group of national parliaments he wishes to reinforce. However, Cameron is perfectly aware that this set of ideas does not achieve the 'holy grail' of British Euroscepticism: a unilateral right for the British parliament to disapply EU laws in the UK. For hardline Conservative Eurosceptics, this is a bottom line, but it is unattainable because once conceded in a single member state, it would lead to the disintegration of the EU.

Freeing business from red tape and turbo-charging free trade deals

Cameron should be able to demonstrate progress on the key policy priorities that the European council has already endorsed for the extension of the single market and new free trade agreements. Promises of reform have of course been made before: yet progress has been disappointingly slow. However this time, in the 2014–19 commission and parliament, there may be more of a favourable political opportunity, particularly given the positive attitudes towards economic reform of the governments that came to power in France and Italy in 2014 under Manuel Valls and Matteo Renzi respectively.

On the question of 'red tape' and regulation, the mindset and policy of the new commission will be of crucial importance. It is therefore a highly significant and positive change from Cameron's perspective that Juncker has appointed Frans Timmermans, the former Dutch foreign minister, as his deputy, with a specific remit to reform regulation. It puts a key British ally, who is totally committed to keeping the UK as a member of the EU, in a crucial position on a subject of huge UK sensitivity.

Nonetheless, there remain critical difficulties arising from a clash of perceptions. In the British Eurosceptic mindset, the European commission and parliament have a single-minded mission to regulate, to stifle business with red tape and to resist the spread of free markets. This is completely at odds with the common continental argument that the biggest problem with the EU is that it has been too uncritical a handmaiden of globalisation and liberalisation. The Eurosceptic perception of Brussels is as an over-mighty agent of bureaucracy and regulation. But this flows from a complete misunderstanding of the difference between a free trade area and the much deeper economic integration that the single market requires. It is because of the UK national interest in a strong competitive single market, underpinned by EU legislation over a broad field of common rules and standards, that previous governments of all parties have traditionally supported the rights of the commission and court to enforce fair rules. The Eurosceptic agenda of repatriation and deregulation, combined with greater discretion for member states, is frankly contrary to this view of the UK national interest. The only way through this clash of perceptions is not to set out on an impossible mission to rip up or repatriate the EU *acquis* (the body of EU law), but rather to ensure that EU laws and regulations are proportional to their purpose and fairly applied in all member countries. This is the Timmermans' agenda, on which Cameron should hope to build.

Power flowing away from Brussels

Across the EU, there is huge support for the principles of subsidiarity and proportionality (power 'flowing back' as Cameron puts it) but not at the expense of the single market's disintegration. The Dutch have advocated the idea of a new interinstitutional agreement between the European council, parliament, and commission on how the competences of the EU will be exercised in the future. The purpose of this exercise would be to reinforce the emphasis on key policy priorities, strengthen the system of legislative impact assessment, give new dynamism to the process of regulatory review of the existing *acquis*, and add real substance to the principles of proportionality and subsidiarity in how the EU acts. Such a move could be significant – and the Timmermans appointment is, from the UK perspective, very good news.

Repatriation of powers, however, requires treaty change and will be much harder to achieve. What might be achievable would be for the European council, representing the heads of government, to agree a declaration, which would not itself amount to a treaty change, but would lay down a set of principles for how it sees the

EU's future institutional development. A model for this would be the Laeken declaration in December 2001, which set the agenda for the convention that followed it. Such a declaration would need to address the reality of an increasingly two-tier EU, with a more closely integrated inner-core eurozone and the existence of a group of member states outside, for whom membership is not in prospect for the foreseeable future. This is already a live issue given the recent debate over whether candidates for EU appointments from non-euro member states could be eligible. At some stage the bigger question will have to be resolved of how legitimate it is for a commission and parliament representing all 28 member states to rule on policies that only concern the 18 member countries of the eurozone. Such a declaration might also provide a vehicle for demonstrating that the EU has moved away from the presumed federalist and centralising ambitions of 'ever-closer union'.

Britain no longer subject to 'ever-closer union'

Cameron has set as an objective that the treaty commitment to 'ever-closer union' should not apply to the UK. Doctoral theses can be written on the legal and practical significance of the reference in the treaties to 'ever-closer union'. The present treaty text which calls for an 'an ever-closer union of the peoples' should be perfectly acceptable to supporters of Britain's EU membership who believe in a united Europe in which the nation states continue to play a leading role, which is neither a federal Europe, nor a centralised Europe. But the sentiment of 'ever-closer union' clearly grates with some as a lingering symbol of a 'United States of Europe' ambition. Paradoxically for Cameron, Blair actually succeeded in removing the phrase 'ever-closer union' from the original draft of the constitutional treaty, but it later reappeared. If Cameron wants Britain to opt out of 'ever-closer union' of the EU member states in a new protocol or declaration, one doubts if our partners would go to the wall opposing it.

Benefit tourism

The Conservatives added curbs on 'benefit tourism' to their list of renegotiation demands in the light of the Ukip's surge in the spring and summer polls of 2013 and the media frenzy over the ending of the UK's transitional controls on free movement of labour from Bulgaria and Romania in January 2014. The evidential basis for believing that abuse of benefits by EU migrants is widespread is weak, if 'abuse' refers to those who come to Britain with no intention of seeking work, but with the purpose of claiming social benefits. Most EU migrants are young people only too keen to work and earn, with a higher employment rate than native citizens of a similar age. Yet claims of benefit tourism strike a chord across the EU. One reason may be that they are a polite proxy for widespread public prejudice against the Roma, who for all kinds of historic cultural reasons integrate as badly into western societies as in the southeast European nations of their origin, where they suffered centuries of harsh discrimination.

Also in the UK the sheer scale of net migration since 2004 has been unprecedented with all the localised pressures that has brought. This has aggravated long-standing social problems. David Cameron sees the issue as 'too many British people untrained and too many without the incentive to work because they can get a better income living on benefits'. What, however, Cameron fails to acknowledge is that large-scale eastern European labour migration has occurred in a decade when wages and standards of living for families in the broad middle of the income distribution have been squeezed and on average have fallen. Most economic research disputes the reality of any general causal relationship; however, it can be no surprise that the public has made the link between the two phenomena. There are clearly some instances of competitive wage undercutting, for example where foreign subcontractors bring over groups of migrant labourers to work at (or even below) the minimum wage or where highly skilled migrants can undermine and outperform pockets of labour monopoly that particular groups have been able to establish and enforce because of previous local labour shortages. Many of the labour market issues that UK citizens experience as a result of migration are mainly ones for national labour market regulation: for example, the setting and enforcement of minimum wages, the abuse of subcontracting, the regulation of zero-hour contracts.

However, in addition in the specific circumstances of the UK, tensions over labour migration reflect the way in which the British social security system has evolved since William Beveridge's 'insurance' model was proposed in the 1940s. Over decades, the British welfare system has prioritised the principle of need over the principle of contribution, in part because generous contributory benefits were judged unaffordable. There is little earnings-related element in unemployment insurance. Tax credits to top up low wages are available universally on the basis of present family income (wherever the rest of the family lives) not on the basis of past contribution. Social housing is allocated on the basis of need and homelessness, not length of stay on a waiting list. Whether or not Britain had seen large-scale labour migration, it is questionable whether the present welfare consensus among the elites, including Labour elites, chimes with the attitudes of the general public, as figures like Frank Field have long argued. But the reality of large-scale labour migration has broken the perception of 'fairness' necessary to underpin any social welfare system.

Finding acceptable solutions to those problems depends on reform of national social security systems to shift entitlements back towards the Beveridge contribution principles. These are not matters the rest of the EU can resolve for the UK, although they can help. Nonetheless, there is political momentum among our EU partners behind the demand for amendments to existing EU legislation to ensure that benefit abuses can be tackled. The European court of justice recently upheld the German authorities' decision to deny benefits to a migrant who had shown no intention of seeking work. David Cameron, supported apparently by the Labour party, wishes to go further in denying migrants who find jobs (not 'scroungers', but hardworking EU citizens) access to the in-work benefits that UK citizens receive, such as tax credits and child benefits. The European commission is open to the idea that the importance of the contributory principle should be more fully recognised in EU directives concerning free movement. Anything, however, that was directly discriminatory in its effect would be a much harder sell to our partners. Numerical controls on internal EU migration are however, an even more difficult proposition.

New controls on vast migrations

Until the October 2014 Conservative party conference, Cameron was careful to confine himself to controls that would apply to new countries joining the EU, not interfere with migration rights for existing EU members. This caution was for good reason. Free movement of labour is one of the founding four freedoms established in the treaty of Rome. The question for any renegotiation is whether this freedom is absolute.

Migration is a huge issue that that affects many member states within the EU; not just the UK, but countries as diverse as Germany and Greece. Internal EU migration has been a massive issue in southern Europe: for example, 1 million Romanians are estimated to be living and working in Italy. In France, there have been periodic demands from the far-right to abandon Schengen and reintroduce national border controls on all forms of migration. In his efforts to win over National Front voters in the second round of the French presidential election in 2012, Nicolas Sarkozy pledged to reinstate national border controls. In the autumn of 2014, Marine Le Pen, the NF leader, demanded action to protect the French borders and prevent the 'floods' of migrants from outside the EU making their way to Calais in their attempt to seek work in the deregulated labour markets of the UK.

Of course because Britain is not a member of the Schengen system and operates its own border controls, it would be practical, in administrative terms, to impose a visa regime on migrants from the rest of the EU (apart from the Irish Republic). But, it is extremely unlikely, given the sensitivity of migration as an issue in other member states, that our EU partners would agree that Britain can breach its free movement obligations under the EU treaties in this way. The politics would be extremely difficult for EU leaders who daily have to face up to political pressures on migration in their own countries. In demanding controls on migration from existing EU member states, David Cameron would therefore be crossing an extremely difficult and dangerous line in his renegotiation demands, and he appears to have recognised this. He would also be putting at risk the rights to free movement that millions of British citizens take full advantage of, including the 2 million British citizens estimated to be resident in other EU member states.

What might be proposed? One possibility is stricter enforcement of existing 'free movement' rights. On the basis of British acceptance of the general principle that there is an absolute right to travel across internal EU borders and an absolute right to work in any member state, it may be possible to obtain the agreement of our EU partners that there is no right to remain beyond a strictly limited period unless migrants demonstrate their ability to support themselves and their families through obtaining and keeping a job.

Cameron also wants 'EU jobseekers to have a job offer before they come here'. This proposal is almost certainly inconsistent with the free movement principles of the EU treaties. Another possibility is the temporary negotiation of 'safeguard clauses' so that in an 'emergency', free movement rights can be restricted. John Major advocated this in a speech he made in support of Britain's EU membership in November 2014. But what would count as an 'emergency'? Who would decide whether on the agreed definition, an 'emergency' existed? And what actions would be required of a member state acting in an 'emergency' to resolve the underlying problem? For instance, this might involve a requirement to direct EU and national budgets to areas of migration stress where public services have come under severe pressure. Labour's proposal for an EU migration fund to deal with the stresses that migration causes is achievable as an extension of the existing role of the EU structural social funds. However, to win the reluctant consent of our partners to such an arrangement, the European commission would have to be the judge and jury of such matters on clearly stated criteria. (Anti-immigration populists would be bound to attack this as an affront to UK national sovereignty). Yet without such provision, governments across the EU would be under constant populist pressure. Such safeguard clauses would not only be complex, bureaucratic and non-communautaire, but in the end unacceptable to our position and ineffective for UK purposes.

None of these actions would significantly reduce internal migration, which is largely driven by economics: while the eurozone is locked in stagnation and huge divergences in living standards between all EU member states remain (and in some cases are growing), the plentiful supply of jobs in the UK's loosely regulated labour market will continue to be a strong magnet. The UK could take domestic action to make its labour market less flexible. But the idea that it can regain full control its borders while remaining a member of the EU is a fantasy. And why, objectively, should it want to, given that internal EU migration has been a considerable economic benefit all round, including to many millions of Britons? To promise to 'solve' the migration problem with temporary 'fixes' that in practice will affect migration flows very little, would simply be to undermine further the public's trust in politics.

British police and courts liberated from unnecessary interference by the European court of human rights

Restrictions on migration raise delicate issues of human rights as well as EU laws and treaties. Yet on a separate but parallel path, the Conservatives at their October 2014 conference affirmed a radically aggressive policy towards British adherence to the European convention on human rights. While protesting their support for the principles of fundamental human rights (to be codified in a new UK Human Rights Act), they insist that the UK parliament should have the sovereign right to overturn the Strasbourg court's rulings. In the eyes of most legal experts, this amounts to effective UK withdrawal from the convention of which the British were founding signatories. This is because the Conservative proposal negates the ECHR's central principle that states subscribing to the charter accept the judgements of a higher sovereign authority – in this case, the European court based in Strasbourg – charged with guaranteeing the application of the principles of the charter to citizens in all member countries. The irony that this would equate Britain with countries like Belarus, and be received gleefully by other oppressors of human rights throughout the world as a justification for their activities, appears totally lost on this policy's advocates.

Strictly speaking, Britain's future adherence to the Strasbourg convention does not relate to the EU at all. Yet British policy on the ECHR would impinge on any EU renegotiation in several ways. First, the EU's own adherence to the ECHR is on the agenda: while all member states presently subscribe to the charter, the question is whether and how the EU as a polity in its own right should do so. Second, the objects and founding principles of the EU treaties implicitly recognise adherence to ECHR principles as does the EU's own charter of fundamental rights now incorporated in the Lisbon treaty. The UK obtained a so-called 'opt-out' from some charter of fundamental rights provisions, but the legal significance of that opt-out is uncertain and questionable. The whole area is surrounded by considerable legal convolution, which few other than a handful of jurists fully understand. Third, there is the question of the jurisdiction of the European court of justice as it applies to the UK, which most Eurosceptics are keen to curb. Human rights considerations have a great bearing on the UK's future participation in the Lisbon treaty's justice and home affairs provisions, from which the present government recently exercised a general opt-out. However, the coalition has opted back in to key measures such as the European arrest warrant: the home secretary and the police and security services are strong advocates and regard this as essential to the UK's ability to counteract terrorism. The extent to which any 'opting back in' automatically involves acceptance of ECJ jurisdiction, and in turn the application of ECHR principles, could prove a technical, but most difficult point in any renegotiation.

THE POLITICS OF A 2017 REFERENDUM

A Martian able to listen in only on the intensity of the political debate in Britain on the European question would imagine that Europe was an issue of burning public interest – perhaps the most important political question of the times, animating discussion around every kitchen table and intruding into every opportunity for social intercourse. The Martian would be wrong. According to all the evidence of opinion research, less than 10 per cent of voters normally place 'Europe' in the top three issues they care about. According to YouGov, only 22 per cent of Ukip supporters think Europe is the most important issue facing the country.

The vast majority of the British public are not fanatical in their opinions of the EU. They are genuine sceptics in a way members of the political class who describe themselves as Eurosceptic often are not. Take the October 2014 poll conducted by Ipsos Mori on whether Britain should stay in or get out of the EU: 56 per cent opted for staying in and 36 per cent for getting out. Mori have been polling the same question since the 1970s. The October 2014 figure was the highest figure supporting British membership since the early 1990s, when both John Major for the Conservatives and Labour under Neil Kinnock and then John Smith were keen to put Britain at the 'heart of Europe'. It was also a turn around since the same question was asked three years before, when 49 per cent wanted to get out and only 41 per cent to stay in. Opposition to the EU in Britain has risen and fallen with the swelling and fading of the eurozone crisis. This replicates previous patterns. In the harsh recession of the early 1980s, the feeling that we should 'get out' was much stronger – by a margin of 65-26 per cent in March 1980.

According to the latest Ipsos Mori survey, it is not the case that a big majority of the public are clamouring for renegotiation of Britain's EU relationship. Of those surveyed, 29 per cent are happy for the relationship to stay the same and a further 14 per cent favour closer European integration, whereas 17 per cent want Britain to leave altogether and 34 per cent to return to an 'economic relationship'. In summary, 43 per cent favour at least the status quo and 51 per cent a move in the direction that Eurosceptics press for. However, of the 34 per cent who favour a less integrated Europe, getting on for half would still choose to 'stay in'.

Some will argue that this presentation of polling data ignores the extent to which immigration is now second only to the economy in the general public's order of concerns. Given the salience of immigration, and the fact that Ukip has gained traction by arguing that Britain can only retain control of its own borders by leaving the EU, this suggests there is much higher potential for an 'out' vote. But what proportion of the public would actually vote in a referendum to come out of Europe in the belief that this would give Britain back control of its borders? There are several reasons for believing that the arguments against this proposition can be won.

First, the countervailing arguments have not yet been fully aired. For example, such a unilateral move would in all likelihood impose unpopular (and possibly heart-rending) constraints on the 'free movement' that UK citizens enjoy across Europe.

Second, withdrawal from the EU could put in jeopardy the present scale of cooperation Britain receives from our EU neighbours, particularly Belgium and France, in enforcing Britain's own national border controls. If Britain leaves the EU, will Belgium and France continue to allow British immigration officials to carry out border entry checks on their territory? Without that cooperation, the

UK problems with asylum control and illegal immigration would be far worse.

Third, public attitudes to immigration are more nuanced than crude polling data suggests. The public would like the numbers of migrants to come down, but this applies to all sources of immigration, not just internal EU migration. At the same time, a recent British social attitudes survey revealed that the public believes migrants should, after an interval of one or two years, be entitled to equal treatment in terms of social benefits and housing, providing they work and settle. The public wants our welfare state to reflect 'contribution' more than it presently does, but not on the basis of nationality, race or ethnicity.

This is part of a wider problem with the European debate that pro-European arguments have yet really to make an impact. Polling and focus group research suggests that the economics of EU membership are seen to be either evenly balanced or negative. The majority do not at present believe pro-European talk of '3m jobs at risk' as a result of loss of unimpeded access to the single market. At present, the public assume trade will not be significantly affected, for the simple reason that our partners have a strong interest in trading freely with us. But whereas over 40 per cent of our trade is with them, only 8 per cent of their trade is with us. So who holds the whip hand in any renegotiation?

Britain has not been able to avoid the economic consequences for our own economy of the eurozone crisis by not being part of the euro. On the face of it, this is an argument for stronger British engagement in the EU to help revive the European economy. Eurosceptics, however, jibe that this amounts to being 'tied to a corpse'. Their alternative may be delusional: that Britain should seek a new economic destiny 'across the open seas', trading with dynamic regions of the global economy without the incubus of EU membership. But pro-Europeans have somehow to counter the argument that British trade will be more successful once freed from the costly 'burden' of unnecessary EU regulations.

The burden of EU regulation is widely believed to be huge in scale, though complaints about it are rarely specified in any detail:

the British debate currently ignores the counterfactual that if there was no EU regulation then new national regulations would be needed in many areas. Small business in particular loathes EU employment as well as health and safety regulation, but whether the general public would share this view if they were made properly aware of its practical content – for example, the potential loss of legal rights to four weeks paid holiday, equal treatment of part-time workers and parental leave – is doubtful.

Equally, arguments that Brexit would diminish Britain's global influence do no presently cut much ice. Post-Iraq and post-Afghanistan, and despite recent turmoil in Ukraine and the Middle East, much of the public would prefer Britain not to get involved in conflicts that are 'none of its business'. As for the proposition that Britain gains increased weight by working with our EU partners, that tends to be dismissed on the argument that our partners are an unreliable lot anyway!

In a referendum there is the potential for these arguments to be turned round. To the extent the UK has done well economically (and had any kind of industrial strategy for the past 30 years) it is because Britain has been successful as a magnet for inward investment that owes much to the fact that it enjoys unimpeded access to the European single market. Foreign-owned firms play a crucial role in many parts of Britain, not simply in the City of London: already there are signs that uncertainty over Britain's EU membership is casting a pall over a much needed investment-led recovery.

In turn, because the European single market is the home market for many British-based businesses, it offers the breadth and depth of scale to enable firms to compete successfully in global markets beyond Europe. And because Britain is in the EU, British-based firms have the bargaining clout of the world's wealthiest economic area behind them in trade disputes with China, India and other rising economic powers. Outside the EU, Britain on its own would lack that clout.

Similarly, in foreign policy, while the present public mood is anti-intervention, this goes along with increasing recognition that we live in a dangerous world, where power is slipping away from the west at a rapid rate. In troubled times, it makes obvious good sense to remain close to neighbours and friends. Leaving the EU would be a very big step into the unknown.

The case for Europe has been put somewhat more strongly since Cameron's Bloomberg speech. His positive tone then rallied public support for Europe and licensed the diminished ranks of British pro-Europeans, particularly in business, to be more vocal in making the case for membership. But given the political pressures on Cameron and the steady drift to a more Eurosceptic agenda of renegotiation, it is naive for pro-Europeans to assume that Cameron can pull off the same renegotiation/referendum manoeuvre that Harold Wilson achieved in 1975. There are crucial differences of circumstance, none of them favourable to pro-European optimism.

In 1975, all the press (with the exception of the small-circulation communist Morning Star) supported a yes vote. Of course the influence of the press has declined since the 1970s, with circulation in sharp decline and the rise of new media. But the press still has an agenda-setting capability that the broadcasters tend to follow – and therefore they still matter. Since the late 1980s, the great majority of the British press has not just been Eurosceptic; on Europe, it has been positively malign. Foreign owners, such as Rupert Murdoch, who see the EU as a high-tax, over-regulated, sclerotic polity not fit for the world of globalisation. These proprietors have consistently provided a platform for a generation of centre-right journalists and commentators determined to uphold the Thatcherite flame. They uphold myths about Margaret Thatcher and Europe that have proved of toxic power inside the Conservative party, for example that all along Thatcher was right about Europe and the pro-Europeans were proved wrong; that the essence of Thatcherism was a virulent anti-Europeanism that in truth she never pursued for much of her period as prime minister; and that her famous Bruges speech was an argument for leaving Europe, when in fact it was an argument for a different kind of reformed Europe. The press proprietors have facilitated the creation of a national myth.

In 1975, business support for the UK's EU membership was crucial. Surveys demonstrate that business today remains strongly in favour of membership, but there are vociferous exceptions, especially among some hedge fund managers in the City who donate significant amounts to the Conservative party. Sometimes this conveys an impression that the City is anti-Europe, when in fact the overwhelming majority in the City see a crucial dimension of its future success as remaining the vibrant financial centre of Europe's single market. As for manufacturing, much is now owned by UK-based foreign companies, who have been reluctant to engage in what they see as domestic politics. This should change. The car industry, much of it now owned by Japanese and Indian companies, would face a 10 per cent tariff on UK exports if Britain left the European Economic Area. The power of business to make its voice heard was shown in the last few days of the Scottish referendum in September 2014. Yet the business message carries significantly less conviction with the public than two generations ago in the wake of a succession of City scandals and the perceived greed of top business executives. Business views matter, but pro-Europeans have to do better than rely on threats.

In 1975, Harold Wilson had a divided Labour party to contend with, just as David Cameron today has a divided Conservative party, but there were crucial differences. The politics of managing a divided government party were easier in 1975; Wilson persuaded a clear majority of the cabinet to back his renegotiated terms, but a narrow majority of Labour MPs and a two-to-one majority of the Labour conference opposed them. Wilson handled this division by proposing an 'agreement to differ' which allowed individual Labour ministers and party members to campaign against the government's recommendation. Could Cameron not do the same?

Cameron faces a much more serious problem in maintaining party unity. In 1975, all the electable contenders for the Wilson succession (Wilson was to retire in March 1976) loyally supported his renegotiation strategy: the bulk of opposition came from the traditional left of the party, still then a minority force in the parliamentary Labour party which still retained the sole constitutional right to elect the party leader. By 2017, if Cameron wins the general election, he will have been prime minister for more than seven years and party leader for more than 12. The manoeuvring for his succession will well and truly have been joined – and the final choice will be made (as Conservative party rules now stand) in a ballot of all party members between the two candidates most favoured by the party's MPs. There would be a great temptation for a leading contender (possibly Boris Johnson) to 'cut and run' from the party leadership and oppose whatever renegotiation deal Cameron is minded to recommend. For Cameron, this could make the politics of carrying his party with him to support any deal he has concluded far more complex than that faced by Wilson.

There is no doubt that were David Cameron to make a firm recommendation in a referendum for continued membership, this would carry some weight. In an age where politics and politicians are deeply tarnished, Cameron carries more respect as prime minister than any other figure in British politics, though the public, at present, likes Ukip's Nigel Farage more. Cameron would have influence with undecided and Conservative voters, just as his intervention in the voting reform referendum in May 2011 proved to have a decisive impact. And his support for our EU membership would almost certainly be backed by the then leaders of Labour and the Liberal Democrats, making for a strong cross-party coalition.

But what will be Cameron's call? Cameron comes from an old-fashioned school of Conservative pragmatism, which believes that, above all else, it is in the national interest that the Conservative party remains united and in power. But every day it is more and more evident that he cannot achieve this objective and keep Britain in the EU at the same time. Hardline anti-Europeanism is only of burning concern to a section of the political class. But in a section of the Conservative party, it really does burn. Traditionally it has comprised an ill-fitting alliance of dogmatic free marketeers, Atlanticist neocons, Westminster sovereigntists and radical libertarians. What has made this motley alliance powerful is the rise of anti-immigration populism. In some ways, this is similar to the late 1960s and early 1970s when Enoch Powell opposed common market membership on sovereigntist grounds, but gained the support of a huge constituency in the country following his 'rivers of blood' speech opposing immigration. What is different, however, between now and then is that Powell had nowhere else to go as a politician in England: in October 1974, the only way he could stay in parliament was through exile to Northern Ireland and the Unionist nomination for South Down. Today, Ukip beckons on the Tories' anti-European flank.

There is a debate among political scientists about how much of the Ukip vote is based on anti-immigration feeling and how much on a more general reaction against 'elite' politics and indeed the wider establishment in our society. For example, according to research by Will Jennings and Gerry Stoker at the University of Southampton, Ukip voters are far more likely than supporters of any other political party to believe that the MMR vaccine is dangerous despite the assurances of the medical establishment to the contrary: nothing at all do with politics, but revealing an attitude towards what the general public are told by people in positions of authority. Voters with this mindset will believe whatever their prejudices tell them about benefit abuse, or immigrants getting preference for social housing, whatever factual evidence is presented to the contrary. If this is the case, 'chasing after Ukip' is likely to prove a forlorn venture for the established parties, because their promises will simply not be believed. The prevalence of this attitude represents, of course, a real challenge to democracy.

On the other hand, polling does suggest that Ukip support has a ceiling. While a sizeable minority reject 'the establishment', the majority prefer politicians who offer credible solutions, not those that play to blind prejudices. This offers hope that an EU referendum can be won. Yet this should not be a cause for complacency in the pro-European camp. The present loss of trust in politicians and of all people in positions of authority in society still poses the most significant risk of Brexit if a referendum is called.

Cameron can only win a referendum at the price of standing up to these pressures and causing what it likely to prove a lasting split in the Conservative party and its natural electorate. At Bloomberg, he made a case for Europe that many wealth creators in Britain would endorse: a case for 'a more flexible, a more adaptable, a more open' European Union. But it is the case for openness that his Ukip defectors fundamentally reject. Among the true believers, the Westminster air is full of the wild talk of a 'reverse takeover' of the Conservative party. The tensions within the Conservative constituency between being the party of the wealth creators and the party that can rally back the anti-migrant populists are becoming unbearable. When it comes to it, will Cameron and Osborne be prepared to recognise this reality and pay the necessary political price in Conservative unity for keeping Britain in the EU? This is the biggest doubt that hangs over Britain's EU membership.

THE UNCERTAINTIES OF THE MAY 2015 GENERAL ELECTION

Cameron may not of course remain prime minister after the May 2015 general election: the lottery of the first-past-the-post voting system in this new era of multi-party politics makes electoral prediction hazardous. The odds have shortened on the Conservatives – perhaps not on their winning an overall majority, but maybe holding onto sufficient seats to form a minority government that will put a European renegotiation at the centre of its programme. This conclusion is based on Britain's continuing economic recovery (though it is yet to raise living standards), the steady erosion of the Labour lead in the opinion polls in 2014, Labour's poor poll ratings on leadership and economic competence, and the respectable Conservative performance in the ballot box in both this May's local and European elections.

An electoral meltdown looks a near-certainty for the Liberal Democrats, but they still might hold a decisive number of seats in a balanced parliament. However, the Conservatives' current coalition partners would have questionable legitimacy as well as capacity to block a referendum on the EU.

Similarly, after the Scottish referendum in September, another intriguing possibility for the Conservatives has opened up: that the Scottish National party win a significant number of seats from Labour in its traditional west of Scotland heartlands that voted yes. This would reverse what up to now has been an acknowledged pro-Labour bias. The Conservatives could then offer the nationalists a deeper version of home rule than Labour would be prepared to match, securing in one bold strategic move both support in parliament for a Europe referendum, and a stronger justification for 'English votes for English laws'.

The big uncertainty is the impact of Ukip. In Britain, the migrations made possible by the democratic miracle of the EU's post-communist enlargement have released the social poisons that have been long festering among groups that feel 'left behind' in British society. Ukip has an extraordinarily powerful appeal to this segment, with its distinctive demographic of older white working-class and lower-middle-class voters who left school at 15 or 16. As Vernon Bogdanor has put it, the 'exam passing classes' who occupy leadership positions in all the main political parties have little understanding for, or empathy with, these voters. On the face of it, the Ukip demographic would seem to do more damage to Labour's traditional working-class support. Yet socio-demographics no longer determine voting behaviour in the way that was once assumed. Analysis suggests that Ukip's greatest appeal (about half of their support in the current polls) is to people who voted Conservative in 2010. People who did not vote then, or voted Liberal Democrat, make up the next largest categories. Ukip supporters may have been Labour 'incliners' once, but their disillusionment with the party stretches some way back.

In the 2009 elections to the European parliament, Ukip came second with over 16 per cent of the vote, but scored only three per cent in the 2010 general election. Having won 27.5 per cent in the 2014 European parliament elections, Ukip still scores in the upper teens in many national opinion polls. No one expects their vote in next May's general election to fall as dramatically as it did between 2009 and 2010. Most analysts think that Ukip looks set to hold a significant share – perhaps half – of its May 2014 vote. This may give them an outside chance of winning a handful of Commons seats where the demographics favour Ukip, particularly in declining coastal towns like Douglas Carswell's Clacton constituency in Essex, and Ramsgate in Kent, which constitutes part of the Thanet South constituency that Nigel Farage will contest. If there are further Conservative defections to Ukip after Mark Reckless and his victory in Rochester and Strood, the oxygen of publicity will sustain Ukip's poll position, as might a further unpredictable byelection.

Yet the Ukip leader, who has so far demonstrated a near-pitch-perfect populist appeal, may begin to make mistakes – as he has done in making an alliance with a Polish fascist in the European parliament. He may fall out with Carswell and Reckless as he has with most other figures that have challenged his dominance over Ukip. Yet the longer Ukip can sustain their presence and impact, the more they will be seen as a credible force. If Ukip start to decline, the Conservatives will be able to intensify the squeeze on their supporters. But the weapons the Conservatives have at their disposal are limited. 'Voting Conservative is the only way to secure a referendum on Europe' is of limited appeal to the half of Ukip supporters who think politicians talk about Europe too much! 'Go to bed with Nigel Farage and end up in the morning with Ed Miliband' did not poll well after David Cameron used it in his conference speech, though it may gain more traction once the public starts to focus on the choice of prime ministers as polling day looms.

However, the largest impact of Ukip before 2015 will be on Conservative MPs. Whatever the truth of the situation, many Conservatives will have become convinced that a significant 'toughening up' of the party's stance on Europe – and the linked issue of internal EU migration – is what stands between them losing or saving their seats. Cameron therefore faces a domestic political firestorm over backbench demands for 'greater clarity' in his EU renegotiation strategy. On how he responds, much could hang for Britain's future in Europe.

WHAT WOULD BE DIFFERENT WITH A LABOUR-LED GOVERNMENT?

What would happen on Europe if Ed Miliband becomes prime minister after May 2015? Ed Miliband has bravely resolved that Labour will not follow suit on Cameron's referendum pledge, but pursue its own agenda of EU 'reform'. Unfortunately (from a pro-European perspective) that does not mean that if Labour wins, Britain's position in Europe is entirely secure.

As Labour approaches the 2015 election its attitudes towards Europe and immigration appear to be heading in opposite directions. Up until now Ed Miliband personally has been brave and resolute on Europe. He faced down those within the shadow cabinet who wanted Labour to match Cameron's pledge of an in/out referendum. Such a move would have been dressed up as a pro-European policy by supporters of our EU membership anxious to resolve 'uncertainty', but in reality its primary political purpose would have been to kill the Europe issue and draw back Eurosceptic votes tempted by Ukip. Ed Miliband rejected the argument for an in/out referendum on the grounds that it would be a terrible distraction from the domestic priorities of an incoming Labour government. But he has also stated without equivocation that he believes Britain's future lies in the EU. He adds that he wants to see real reform in Europe, but on the basis of a settled view, as a social democrat, that we should be members and we will stay members. He appears to recognise that the EU represents a level of governance 'beyond the nation state' that is an essential tool of a progressive government determined to rise to the challenges of globalisation. He has appointed Pat McFadden, the former business minister, to make the case for Europe and at the same time devise and pursue a credible Labour agenda of EU reform.

On immigration, however, the Labour position is more opaque, defensive and potentially worrying. Following the success of Ukip in the European parliament elections of May 2014, influential voices within Labour's ranks, began to argue that the party needs to listen to 'our people', who are thought to have defected to Ukip in significant numbers. This is thinly disguised code for the party toughening its stance on eastern European migration in response to pressure from disgruntled voters. Labour has put together a defensive policy package on migration. Labour is right to point to problems of employer exploitation of migrant labour: wage undercutting and the abuse of labour-only sub-contractors. It makes sense to call for stronger incentives for migrants to learn English in order to ease social integration. Labour also calls for strengthening controls at the border in order to check 'exit' as well as 'entry' so that the extent of the problem of illegal immigration can be better estimated, though the consequence could well be to reinforce public contempt for the impotence of government, rather than offer any solution to the 'problem'.

Labour is also right that, in order to maintain public confidence in the social security system, the issue of so-called benefit tourism needs to be addressed. But this is where the presentation of policy runs into serious problems. No doubt there are some problems of abuse of the benefits system among migrants – but the employment rate among those of working age is much higher among migrants than in the native population. Labour should be prepared to acknowledge that plain fact: otherwise a constant emphasis on so-called benefit tourism simply encourages disgraceful scapegoating of migrants and their families.

More generally, Labour is at present failing to address the issue of migration in its proper context. All politicians, including Labour ones, are reluctant to acknowledge that migrants have made, and continue to make, a huge positive contribution to the British economy and public finances, as well as meeting labour shortages in construction and essential services, such as social care. There may be genuine issues of cultural assimilation of migrants, though it is difficult to understand why these should apply more to hard working eastern Europeans than to earlier waves of south Asian, African and Caribbean migration. The fact is that there is little hard evidence that migration has had general negative effects; Labour should be prepared to say so. The 'problem of migration' is often a proxy for the inadequacy of social provision, such as decent housing to rent. But housing shortages are not the fault of migrants, but a failure of wider housing policy: without the benefit of the tax contribution that migrants make to the British exchequer, the state would be in a weaker position in the present age of austerity to address these wider social problems.

Britain needs a new language of honesty about migration, but Labour, like the Conservatives, is unwilling to address the facts. The focus groups warn politicians that 'telling the truth about migration' is seen as attacking Ukip supporters and will therefore lose votes – yet this is an abnegation of political leadership. And on the issue of European migration absence of leadership can lead only in one direction. If politicians tacitly accept the Ukip argument that eastern European migration is a massive problem that needs to be curbed, then the only possibility of a long-term solution is to halt the inward migrant flow is to break the UK's legal obligations under the 'free movement' principles of the EU treaties.

To impose numerical controls at the UK border on internal EU migration would involve a return to some system of visas and work permits. This would be incompatible with our continued EU membership and have unavoidable and incalculable consequences for the millions of British citizens who travel, live, work, study and retire on the continent. Yet the main problem with this policy is not that it is anti-Europe and its logic will drive Britain out of the European

Union, but that it is wrong. Not only would it be inconsistent with a fundamental principle of EU membership, it would even more importantly make Britain a poorer, more narrow-minded and inward looking country – just the opposite of the 'openness to the world' which should be the hallmark of Britain's success in the global age.

The questions have also to be seen in the post-2015 political context if there is a Labour government after May. Consider the impact of election defeat on the Conservatives. David Cameron's failure in the general election to keep the Conservatives in office would be his death knell as Conservative leader. Given that in all likelihood, the size of the vote for Ukip would be blamed for the Conservatives' defeat, his successor, would probably have struck a more Eurosceptic and anti-immigration note in order to gain the party leadership. Certainly candidates for the Conservative leadership would be under intense pressure from the right of the party to make an unambiguous commitment to EU withdrawal, and/or the imposition of border controls on EU internal migration, with, or possibly even without, a referendum. It would be up to the new Conservative leader to decide whether to attempt to nuance that position, and leave the door open to continued support for EU membership, or give in to pressure from the populist right. Either option would strengthen party divisions. But bold resistance to the rightward drift could possibly lead to further defections by Conservative MPs to Ukip, depending on how credible Ukip remain after the general election.

In the short term, Conservative splits over Europe might play to Labour's advantage – but in truth they pose an existential choice for the Labour party. Governing Britain in the next parliament will not be easy. The short-term bounce back in the economy has masked the depth of the underlying problems: the huge remaining fiscal deficit, a weak balance of payments, and nugatory productivity growth. The pro-investment, pro-growth fiscal consolidation that Britain still requires will involve painful and politically unpopular spending cuts and tax rises. Any Labour government may well have a weak parliamentary position. It may not have an overall majority at all. And if it has one, there will be major problem with rebel MPs opposing tough economic measures from within Labour's own ranks. Even if there is a minority Labour government, there may be a pro-EU referendum majority in the House of Commons.

An increasingly unpopular and possibly divided Labour government could face a more strongly anti-European, anti-immigration Conservative party, possibly competing with a strengthened Ukip, who would then be well placed to pick up disillusioned Labour support, especially among working-class voters in the Labour's north of England heartlands. Immigration is likely to remain the issue that will test Labour the most.

To pose stark binary choices always risks exaggeration; however, Labour in government will face a fundamental choice about what kind of party it is and what electoral strategy it should pursue. Essentially, it will be forced to choose between advocating a social democracy of the closed nation state or defending an open society. If Labour is to follow the logic of the 'open society', it needs to stop obsessing about the loss to Ukip of what may be, if not largely mythical, at least a greatly reducing blue-collar, traditional 'core' vote. Labour under Ed Miliband has based its electoral strategy on winning back 'core' blue-collar voters, who, many argue, 'Blair lost to the party'. Miliband and his allies may be very circumspect about moving back to an 'open society' strategy that potentially appeals to the 'centre ground'. This is not to say Labour should surrender to a naive multiculturalism. Immigration needs controls. The public has to have confidence rules will be enforced. Integration has to be real. But in a globalised world, there will be more immigration. And in the EU it is a two-way street. This is the only credible way forward for progressive politics.

Today, Labour should frame its policy approach in the light of Britain's continuing transformation into a knowledge and service economy with a highly diverse social composition. In the process, Labour would also strengthen its appeal among the business community and middle-class professionals, many of whom are instinctive centre-ground Liberal Democrat and Conservative 'incliners'. Such a pitch to the centre could be the basis of a new progressive consensus in which a modern policy for growth, based on a pro-business industrial activism and a meaningful devolution of power to English cities and regions was combined with a fairer approach to austerity in which taxes (especially new taxes on wealth and property) bear a larger share of the burden of adjustment. There would still be a need for drastic spending cuts with large losses of jobs in parts of the public sector and also tough decisions on welfare, especially for the older-age groups that the coalition has protected at the expense of young families and the working poor. But without a rigorous approach to priorities, Labour will be unable to find the increased resources necessary to fund growing health and social care needs and extend educational opportunities for those with poor life chances. Instead of focusing solely on winning majorities at Westminster, Labour should demonstrate its willingness to work with the grain of multi-level governance. The devolution of power in England would be part of a new constitutional settlement as we move to a federal Britain capable of rebalancing political power as well as economic dynamism, away from its present London and Whitehall dominance.

A Labour policy for European reform should be a natural fit with this broader agenda. Labour should not revert back to trying to avoid the European question and then responding opportunistically when it finds Europe impossible to dodge. Labour needs here to develop its own reform programme, not offer a pale imitation of David Cameron's. This should be based on the following principles:

1. An EU-wide programme of coordinated cross-border and domestic investments to break the stranglehold of deflation and austerity. This would focus on transport, energy and digital infrastructure enabling the EU to reach its target for a 40 per cent reduction in carbon emissions by 2030. This would be financed by a mix of increased lending from the European Investment Bank, innovative EU project bonds, and nimble deployment of structural funds.
2. A new European initiative on tax cooperation to ensure large firms in Europe pay their fair share of corporate taxes and

wealthy individuals cannot escape their obligations through tax havens.

3. A drive for European growth exploiting the potential for cross-border research and cooperation; focusing the EU budget on clear growth priorities, not wasteful spending; deepening the single market in digital, energy and services, balanced by appropriate and proportional regulation at EU level; and vigorously pursuing free and fair trade deals.

4. Support for the principle of a capital markets union that offers fast-growing firms new sources of finance for growth and liberates enterprise from the grip of a failing banking system.

5. A new emphasis on social Europe to ensure every member state adopts a decent minimum wage; to focus the EU social fund single-mindedly on tackling youth unemployment through a common EU youth guarantee; to open up labour markets but protect workers against fears of social dumping; and to reform migration rules.

6. A commitment to create a European defence industry that will meet genuine military procurement needs at significantly lower cost.

7. A commitment to strengthen Europe's common borders, co-ordinate aid to countries that are the sources of migratory pressure, and deepen (not weaken) police and security cooperation.

8. A senior British minister for Europe held accountable to the House of Commons for the policies Britain pursues in the council of ministers.

9. A stronger role for national parliaments in vetting and approving EU policies.

10. A drive to reduce the regulatory burdens of the existing EU *acquis*, simplify EU laws, and ensure the principles of subsidiarity and proportionality are fully adhered to in future.

This should be seen as a considered programme for 'Europeanising' Britain's political economy, which would involve a much broader focus than the normal, economically liberal British concept of 'EU reform'. Liberalisation must happen, but in a broader growth-oriented, environmentally friendly and socially inclusive context.

If Labour fails to be bold on Europe and immigration, the risk is that with a combination of Conservative moves even further to the right on Europe, a weak and unpopular Labour government, and Ukip pitching itself as the main opposition to Labour in many working-class constituencies, the future of Britain's place in Europe would then depend on the even more unpredictable outcome of the general election following 2015, which may come uncomfortably sooner than Labour would like to think.

CONCLUSION

The first half of 2015 will be very difficult for pro-Europeans. Cameron will be constantly on manoeuvres: to convince an impossible party that he is serious about renegotiation, and to try to protect himself against further defections of MPs and voters to Ukip. To win the space for the election campaign against Labour they want to fight, the Conservative leadership will indulge in craven appeasement of Tory Eurosceptic opinion. The risk is that Cameron goes too far – to the point where the rest of Europe begins to believe there is absolutely no point in indulging his planned renegotiation for he has gone beyond anything the others can possibly give.

Yet as long as his own will to keep Britain in the EU remains firm – and this is by no means certain – the task should not be impossible. Should Cameron stay prime minister after 2015, the post-election battle in the Conservative party will be fascinating to watch. But it is difficult to see how a significant split in the Conservative parliamentary party on any conceivable set of renegotiated terms can be avoided.

Current polling suggests that despite the present Ukip surge, a referendum on staying in the EU can be won. But it is unlikely to lance the boil of Euroscepticism in the British body politic. The bigger impact of any referendum may be on the structure of our politics, if the continuing strength of Ukip combined with a Conservative split leads to realignment on the right of British politics.

However, there remains the horrible risk that the politics becomes just too difficult and, in terms of our EU membership, it might all go badly wrong. David Cameron no longer looks, as he did at the time of his Bloomberg speech in January 2013, the best chance of keeping Britain in the EU. The future of Britain's EU membership is no longer safe in Cameron's hands.